Sticky Notes
Volume I

Trinette Collier

Printed in the United States of America

Cover design by Elaina Lee.
Page layout by FreedomInk Publishing.
Initial edit by FreedomInk Publishing.
Final proof by Trinette Collier &
Katandra Jackson Nunnally.

First Printing, 2016

ISBN 978-0-9861001-5-4

FreedomInk Publishing
P O Box 1093
Reidsville, Georgia 30453

www.freedomink365.com

Dedication

Sticky Notes is dedicated to all of the DEDICATED Educators across the world. This task is not easy but it is rewarding! Continue teaching from the heart and you will make a difference.

With Love,

Ms. Collier

Sticky Notes
Volume I

Trinette Collier

<u>Testing Week Rituals</u>

"My grandmamma told me to praise the Lord when I do my test so I can pass. I sure do hope I pass 'cause I praised Him on that first day!"

~1st Grade

<u>Just Checking On the Teacher</u>

Student: "You still mad teacher?"

Teacher: "No sweetie, I don't like being mad or sad."

Student: "Good!"

She then proceeds to yell out to the class, "She ain't mad no mo'!"

~1ˢᵗ Grade

Current Events

Student with the name Trayvon enters the room... Later that day, a few students start chanting "Travon Martin! Travon Martin!"

Birthdays Are Golden!

Student: "I can't wait! My birthday is tomorrow!"

Teacher: "Great! I'm excited for you. Birthdays are really cool!"

Student: "But I don't understand it. Usually my birthday is August 26th, but I'm gonna celebrate it tomorrow!"

The date was March 20th!

~2nd Grade

<u>Teachers Are Creatures Too!</u>

Student: "I'm drawing a picture of you Ms. Collier!"

Teacher: "What is that?"

Student: "A bat surfing! You surfing Ms. Collier"

Teacher: "Ohhhhh, ok!"

~1st Grade

<u>Don't Forget Teachers</u>

Student: "I'm gonna tell my daddy to put your face and mine on my birthday cake!

Teacher: "Why?"

Student: "Cause I like you! Duhhhhh!!!"

A Vote for William is a Vote for a Messed up Bank Account

I have been designated as the Advisor for the Student Council and it's election time! A meeting is called with all 4th and 5th grade students who are interested in campaigning for office. Handouts are distributed and directives are given. If you want to run for office, you need to prepare two creative 22 x 28 posters identifying your full name, potential office and a slogan. You must also prepare a 1 minute persuasive speech to present to the entire student body detailing the top three characteristics that make you the best candidate for the position. The students are nervous and excited, all in one! They are bouncing ideas off each other about preparing their speeches and designing their posters. William, a 5th grade student, rolls over to me in his electric wheelchair. He asks for more information about the responsibilities for the Treasurer. He needs me to break it down. "Okay, as Treasurer, you have to be able to count people and count money. You have to have really sharp math skills and you have to know all of your multiplication facts."

William's disposition crumbles as he lowers his head and admits, "I can't do no math." I know I'm supposed to inspire and motivate but all I could do was think to myself "Well, why you wanna be the Treasurer, son?"

I look into his tear-filled eyes and ask, "So, what are you going to do?"

He manages to mumble, "I guess I'll just still run for Treasurer. Maybe my friends will vote for me anyway."

Oh. Okay William.

~Kindergarten

<u>Kinesthetic Learning</u>

Student: "I love touching iPhones!"

Teacher: "Why?"

Student: "Because I can touch it! I can't wait till I get grown, I'mma touch it all day with my friends!"

~5th Grade
Call Him!

Teacher: "Can you please just finish your work?"

Student: Throws his hands up and yells, "JESUS!"

~1ˢᵗ Grade
<u>Well…</u>

Teacher: "Class, give me some words that begin with the letter Mm"

Student: "BLOODY MARY! My momma got that!"

~1st Grade
Teachers Never Stop!

Teacher: "Ok, you guys let's get ready for some science!"

Male Student: "Aww man, I thought we was finished!"

Female student: "No, yall know she gotta teach us every thang 'cuz she the teacher!"

~1st Grade

<u>Teachers Have Feelings Too!</u>

The students saw a picture of me during my college days.

Student #1: "You were skinny Ms.Collier! What happened to you?!"

Student #2: "Duh! She been eating!"

Student #3: "What happened to your thighs?!"

Student #1: "What happened to THAT MS. COLLIER?!"

~Self-esteem gone out the window.

~Pre K

The Little People

Go back with me to the fall of 1996. I was teaching a Pre-Kindergarten class with 4 year olds at a private daycare. Under the High Scope Program, creative movement for 45 minutes was a mandate. So, being the compliant teacher that I am, I pulled out the record player and turned up the volume. Now, this wasn't just any ole' music. It was Greg and Steve's "The World is a Rainbow" ... and it was an ALBUM! As the students danced around, hugged each other, and sang with the artists, Mister eyed the record player with a look of bewilderment. He slowly walked over to me, eyes glued to that record player.

Then he whispers, "Teacher, I know what that is."

"Okay Mister, you do?"

"Yes! You put that little stick on top and then the little people inside the box start singing!"

"HAHAHAHAHA! YES, THEY DO, MISTER! YES, THEY DO!"

~5th Grade

English...

Teacher: "Get the dictionary and write your definitions, starting with the letter A."

Student: "Man!!! Can I get another dictionary, this one is full of English?"

Teacher: "Sure!"

Distractions and Excuses Go Away!
Come Again...

Well, DON'T COME BACK!

I need a pencil. My pencil broke. I need an eraser. He took my pencil. I need some paper. I forgot my homework. My Mama didn't put it in my book bag. My book bag too heavy. My book bag broke. I didn't bring my book bag. My Mama didn't sign it. My Mama didn't come home last night. My head hurt. My fingers hurt. My nose hurt. My stomach hurt. My back hurt. My leg hurt. My eye hurt. My teeth hurt. It's too hard. It's too easy. It's too much. It's not enough. I already did this. I don't know how to do this. She looking on my paper. She stealing my answers.

He telling me the answer. I'm hungry. I'm full. She sneaking and eating. He got food in his desk. She chewing bubble gum. He got a cell phone. He brought a toy. He looking at me. She talking about me. He making noises. He humming. She singing. He burping. She farting. My Grandma said she was gone help me. My grandma said she was gone come get me early. Is it time to go home?

The New Student

As the students entered the cafeteria for breakfast, I greeted each of them with a smile and a "Good Morning"! Some smiled back. Some spoke. Others just brushed on by. Now there was one little fella who immediately caught my attention. Maybe it was the fact that he wasn't wearing the school uniform. Perhaps it was because he appeared to be all of 2 years old! So I asked the little fella to step over to the side. He did... And was followed by, apparently, his big brother. I asked why he wasn't wearing his uniform. He shrugged his shoulders. I asked who his teacher was. He shrugged his shoulders. I asked if he was hungry and he began to nod his head ferociously. I looked at the big brother, who informed me that he was 6 years old in the 1st grade, and I asked why his brother wasn't wearing the school uniform. He pointedly responded, "He ain't got na'an." Oh. Okay. So I asked big brother who his teacher was and he emphatically responded, "He on't go here." Oh. Okay. I then asked big brother why was the little fella at our school if he didn't go here. He responded, "My Mama told me to bring him." I know, I know, I should've just left it at that, gave the little fella some breakfast and placed him in the Pre-K class until the end of the day. But Nooooooo, I had to call Mama. I mean, surely she's concerned about where her toddler is, right?

Ring Ring Ring! Ring Ring Ring! Ring Ring Ring! (Trina and Rick Ross greet me for like the whole song.) Then I hear her sultry, seductive voice...

"Yeaaaah. Dis Red. You know what to do. LOL..."

"Good Morning Ms. Red. This is Dr. Pie from the Elementary School where you have to be at least 4 years old to attend. We have Little Fella here and need you to come pick him up immediately. We look forward to seeing you within the next 30 minutes. 5 minutes pass. 10 minutes pass. 15 minutes pass. Then I am summoned to the office because I have a phone call.

"Good Morning! This is Dr. Pie, how may I help you?"

"Yeaaaah. Dis Red. You called me?"

"Yes. We have Little Fella here in the front office waiting for you to come pick him up."

She then goes off! "I gotta come all the way up to that school? I'ma git Big Brother! I told him to drop Little Fella off at the neighbor 'partment. Now I gotta git up! I'ma git both of them!" She sucks her teeth and then sighs, "Here I come!"

Just Throw the Newspapers Away

I try to expose the children to a plethora of resources and often utilize supplies and materials alongside the regular textbooks. One particular day as we're looking at the newspaper, the title of an article reads, "For 90-year-old veteran, high school graduation caps a life well-lived."

To build background knowledge, I know it's important to define key terms. I ask, "Who can define veteran?" The young lady raises her hand confidently and says, "The kind of people who don't eat meat."

"Ummmm, good try, but that is a VEG-E-TAR-I-AN." I go on to give clues. "Think about it. There is a holiday that we celebrate called Veteran's Day and we decorate everything with American flags and red, white and blue. Who are we celebrating?" The students are completely baffled! One kid yells out "When that holiday is?" So I just tell them... "A veteran is someone who has served in the Armed Forces. Next question. Before we actually read the article, answer this. Why do you think the man was 90 years old and just now graduating from high school?" I should've known to call on someone else when this one student intensely waved his hand and started bouncing up and down in his seat. But nooooo, I had to call on him.

"Yes, Victor, why do you think it took the man 90 years to graduate from high school?"

Victor replies, "It probably just took him a real real long time to get it."

"Oh. Okay. Everybody just ball up your newspapers and throw 'em in the garbage! Just throw 'em away!!!"

~1st Grade

Out of the Mouths of Babes

As I struggled trying to get a word out, the student yelled "Ms. Collier, you getting too old to teach!"

I knew that was my sign... Out of the mouths of babes!

You Want My Child to Do What?

I've been called into the Principal's office because a parent has some 'concerns'. Okay. Let's hear it. The parent looks at the Principal and holds up the handout I'd distributed to her 3rd grader the previous day. The handout provides directions for Visual Display and Oral Presentation #1. The objectives are listed. The necessary materials are identified. The steps to complete the assignment (both display and speech) are noted. In addition, the scoring rubric is included to serve as a checklist. Mom begins by shouting, "I ain't buying no poster!" The Principal assures Mom that he will give her a poster. Then Mom says, "I ain't got no markers!" The Principal calmly assures the Mom that he will give her a pack of markers. Mom looks at me and lashes out, "I don't know why you giving her this project!" I refer to the standards required to successfully complete 3rd grade. I then convey the connection between the standards and the task. Mom barks, "Well, I don't know why it gotta be so much!" I serenely assert that this is a creative means of addressing the standards in a hands-on fashion where the students will remember the process and have firsthand knowledge of how to properly prepare for presentations. They also get to use a plethora of skills to demonstrate knowledge and understanding; opposed to the traditional, boring paper/pencil test. Mom yells, "You just come up in here thinking you are all that!" I stand, look at the Principal, look at Mom and say, "I'm going back to teach my students now." (Was I wrong for walking out?)

~Dr. Pie

No Time for Conference Time

It's report card time! Time to schedule Parent- Teacher conferences. Who shows up on the wrong day at the wrong time? None other than Ms. Pat. She barges in and demands that I "tell her all about lil man." Okay.

As indicated on the report card, lil man has earned all Ds in all subject areas. I explain that the Ds are not a true reflection of his comprehension, rather a lack of motivation. I then go on to explain my plan of action to increase motivation and time on task as well as share some things she can do and say at home to offer encouragement. Mom interrupts and clarifies that she got business to take care of and making her hair

appointment on time is definitely one!
She snatched up the report card and
told me on her way out, "I will talk to
you later!" Oh. Okay. Thank you.

~Dr. Pie

<u>Pick Up My What???</u>

The breakfast monitor stands on the stage, speaks into the microphone and tells the students to eat and use their inside voices. Needless to say, their voices raise and her level of frustration does as well. She screams into the microphone... "ALRIGHT YOU KIDS! PUT YO TRAYS UP! DUMP YO MILK! TOSS YO SPORKS! LINE UP!!!"

Oh, wow. Did she just say 'SPORK?' (A SPORK is the cross between a spoon and a fork.) New vocabulary for the day!

1st Grade

Use What You Got!

I have the 'Rock' eyebrow and I raised it one day to get their attention.

Student: "Yall see that eyebrow up? That means she ain't happy!"

Needless to say, all of the students got really quiet, quickly!

~1st Grade

Winning!

Teacher asking the students: "Where do you like to go?"

Student #1: "To the casino!" While slapping his hands together!

~1st Grade
First day of school

Male student: "I just knew I would be
in your classroom last year!
I just knew it!"

Ms. Collier: "How did you know that?"

Student: "Because I just knew it!"

Ms. Collier: "You didn't see me."

Student: "Yes I did! When you went to
the office in the hallway!
I just knew it!"
He smiled the entire day!

~Dr. Pie's 1st Grade
Impromptu Sex Education

We leave the cafeteria and I instruct the students to walk around the field to help their lunch digest. Halfway around the field, I see a group of guys huddled together analyzing something on the ground. My first thought was that it was a dead bird or perhaps some dog feces... 'Cause you know things like that intrigue the boys. All of a sudden, Earl takes off running towards me. Bending over and out of breath, he manages to confess, "Dr. Pie, there's a condom over there... And it's been used!"

1ˢᵗ Grade

They Call Me Miss Call!

Male Student: "I'mma call you Miss Call because I can't say dat other you said!"

Ms. Collier: "It's Ms. Coll-ier." (slowly pronouncing it)

Student: "I just can't say it, can I call you Miss Call?"

Ms. Collier: "Ok, just for today!"

Student: "Well, I don't know, I'll try!"

~1st Grade

Time to Go!

Female Student: "You about to leave?"

Ms. Collier: "No, why are you asking that?"

Student: "Because I'm ready to go home! This school take too long!"

It was 1:30 pm.

The New Campaign

Why is it that these little kids say whatever is on their minds? "Yo feet stank! Yo butt on fire! Yo breath kickin!" It doesn't matter if I am in the middle of the lesson or if the students are working quietly and independently. They could care even less if there is a guest in the room. My colleague decided to implement a new campaign. He calls it, "Think it... BUT DON'T SAY IT!" As teachers, we have little control over what goes on in the minds of these students, however, we have taken an oath to encourage them to carefully consider what comes out of their mouths. Now, sometimes what they say is so accurate it ain't funny! But again, we are running a school.

There must be some order. So remember, no matter how true, how funny, how real: THINK IT... BUT DON'T SAY IT!

~Dr. Pie

Data Meeting

As teachers, we do something called Progress Monitoring. This simply means that somebody created a fancy form and requires us to document the results from weekly assessments on students who are at-risk of failing and/or performing below level.

Data meetings are scheduled once a month for a team of educators to collaborate on the best practices and interventions necessary to ensure that no child is left behind. In theory, the interventions "work" and the targeted students get the additional, intensive instruction needed to bridge the gaps.

Well, this team of administrators, counselors, psychologists and teachers work diligently to determine why the students are performing below grade level and how to make the most gains in the least amount of time.

I'm sitting here reviewing the facts: Johnny is in the 5th grade. He reads on a 1st grade level. The standardized test he will take in less than 2 months assesses his knowledge in reading, grammar, math and science. All of the material is written on the 5th grade level. Soooo, even if Johnny does know how to multiply and divide, the word problems will be interpreted as a foreign language and the chances of Johnny passing the math section are slim to none. And again, you want the data to depict what?

~Dr. Pie

~1st Grade
Writing Sentences

Student #1: "That's why I don't like flying planes!"

Ms. Collier: "Why not?"

Student: "It's raining, lightning…"

Student #2 jumps in: "BUT THEY GOT FOOD!"

Don't Work... Don't Eat

I plead with the students to work effectively and efficiently. I beg them to do their best and answer every question. I convey to them that even when they are not 100% certain about a response, an educated guess is better than nothing. And then there is my second period class. They come to me right before lunch. No matter how well my instruction, how engaging my lessons or how much weight an assignment carries, these students don't give a care. There simply is no intrinsic motivation to put forth their best effort. They either half do work, do it wrong or don't do it at all. With that being said, I developed a new classroom policy...

Don't Work? Don't Eat!

I am so proud to announce that all 15 of my students in the second period have earned A's for the semester!

~Dr. Pie

~1st Grade

BLL

Male Student yells out during the middle of a lesson
"My daddy got a Bugotti, Lamborgini, and a Limo!"

~1st Grade
My Name is Ms. COLLIER!

Student #1: "Teacher!"

Student #2: "Her name not teacher!
It's Miss Carter!"

~1st Grade

<u>Just Because...</u>

In the middle of testing

Ms. Collier: "Sweetheart, what are you doing?"

Female Student: "I'm swinging my feet!" Like duhh!

~1st Grade
<u>No Cuss Zone</u>

Student: "Teacher! He need to tell his mom to not cuss in front of him so he don't cuss. Every time my momma cuss, I walk to my room 'cuz I don't want to cuss!"

Ms. Collier: "That's right darling, this is a no cussing zone!"

~1st Grade
<u>Asking vs. Telling</u>

During diagnostic testing after reading instructions, I asked if there were any questions.

Student: "I have a question..."

Ms. Collier: "Yes sweetie, what is it?"

Student: "This is hard!"

~1st Grade
Hidden Message

Ms. Collier: "Give me 'S' words."
Students all yell out: "Summer, skate, slither, slime, snake, star, SOUL!"
Teacher: "Soul?"
Student #1: "Yeah, the human soul!"

~1st Grade

S-P-E-L-L-I-N-G

Student: "Teacher! I can spell Frozen!"

Ms. Collier: "Ok, great! Spell it…"

Student: "O-E- Z- R- N- F"

Teacher: ☺

~1st Grade
Kids Know Best

I sneezed 4x in a row...

Student: "I'mma get you something to make you sick and I'mma get you something to make us proud and I'mma get you something to make you nice with a balloon! And nobody betta not take it off your desk!"

I was looking confused! I thought I was nice and sweet! Oh well, kids know best!

~1st Grade

I'm Pretty!

In the middle of a great lesson, a student raises his hand with excitement! I'm excited because I'm thinking he is responding to the lesson. So I answer him...

Student: "I like yo' dress and shoes! You look pretty!"

So that one comment, sparks the other 17 compliments for the next 20 minutes.

~1st Grade

Gee... Thanks!

Writing and reading a sentence on the board. "My name is Ms. Collier."

Student #1: "What's your real name?"

Teacher: "Ms. Collier"

Student #1: "No! Your name at home?"

Student #2: "Is it Mom?"

Teacher: "No..."

Student #3: "She ain't got no children!"

~1st Grade

<u>Mister Clean</u>

Male student: "Can I please (he stressed it) give everybody hand sanitizer?"

Teacher: "Why?"

Student: "They need to be clean!"

~1st Grade

Monday-Friday

Ms. Collier: "Good morning! Welcome back! Where were you Friday?"

Male student: "Home!"

Teacher: "Why?"

Student: "I was sleepy so I didn't feel like getting up!"

Ms. Collier: "Well, I really need you to come to school on Mondays, Tuesdays, Wednesdays, Thursdays AND Fridays!"

Student: "But why?"

Ms. Collier: "Because we really need you! You are a great learner!

So is it a deal?"

Student: "OK"...with such disappointment!

~1st Grade

<u>Weekly Agendas</u>

Teacher: "Please make sure to give these papers to your Mom, Dad, Grandparents or Aunts."

Male student: "I ain't got no daddy!"

Female Student: "YES you do! His name is Steve!"

Male student: "Steve don't live with us no more! We got rid of him! I don't know my new daddy!"

Female student: "OHHHHHHHHH!"

~1st Grade
Blood Advice

Student: "Just lick your blood so it can go back in your body so you won't lose any more!"

~1st Grade

Girls!

Male student: "Teacher! She said she
my girlfriend! What the hell!"

Ms. Collier: Yelling out his name,
"What did you say?!"

Student: "She said she my girlfriend!
What the hell!"

~1st Grade
Friday Funny

I stood in the front of the line to model how our line should look; In the square with your hands behind your back and very quiet. Well, as we stood there, I felt something a bit heavy on the top of my bottom...a female child behind me rested her head on my toosh! There was a male teacher standing in the doorway who fell out laughing!! I couldn't do anything but laugh myself!

~1st Grade
Just Buy More!

Student: "Teacher, my momma don't have any money for the snack store. She gotta buy more money!"

Ms. Collier: "Yeah, I understand sweetie, I gotta buy some more too!"
☺

~1st Grade
The 'L' Word

Student: "Ooooweee Teacher! He just said the L word!"

Teacher: "What word?"

Student: "LIE!"

~1st Grade

Handle That!

Serious male student (referring to another student): "Ms. Collier, he getting out of control!" As if to tell me that I need to handle that!

~1st Grade

<u>1st Grade Reading</u>

We were reading Richard Wright and the Library Card, so of course the discussions are about black and white people, segregation, and equal rights.

Student #1: "We black?"

Ms. Collier: "Yes, we are African Americans with brown skin."

Student: "Why?
We supposed to be black!"

So then, the class erupts into a million and one questions about how come our skin doesn't look like the color black.

Ms. Collier: "Class, let's get focused! Bring it back so that we can complete the story."

Student #2: "Ok! Get all this African American stuff out of my head and put black back in!"

The Interview!

Student comes in everyday to chat with me. She asks all the questions that a 1st grader wants to know. The infamous questions such as:

"Do you have any kids? Do you have a husband? Do you have a dog?"

After answering "No" to all 3, she gasped so frantically that I almost cried!

She said: "WHATTTTTT! None of those?!"

I just smiled and said "Soon hunny!"

~1st Grade
Just a minute...

Teacher: "Hey my babies! I really want to talk to you all but remember, this is my morning moment. Give me about 5 more minutes and I'm all yours!

Student #1: "That's right! Yall know better! She gotta get herself together so she can keep her job!"

Student #2: "She gotta get all her stuff together so she can teach us right!"

I simply dropped my pencil!

~1st Grade
Common sense...

Two female students fighting
over a hair bead.

Male student yells out: "Yall gotta get
some common sense!"

I didn't have to say a word!

~1st Grade
Guided Reading

Teacher: "Larry, please read."

Student #1: "Ms. Collier, he can't do it because he don't pay attention!"

Student #2: "I told him though!"

~1st Grade
<u>Time</u>

Student #1: "Ms. Collier, is it lunch time yet?"

Ms. Collier: "No, not yet."

Student #2: "Well, what time is it?"

Ms. Collier: "It's 10:40 am."

And then I begin to provide a mini lesson on time, short hand & long hand, minutes, hours...

Student #2 looks at me like ok, that's great and all... Then proceeds to ask, "Well, can you just turn it to lunch time?"

~1st Grade
I am Smart!

Student #1: "Ms. Collier thinks she smart!"

Other students: "Oooooo! She is! Why you think she teaching us!"

Students: "Ooooooo"

As the crowd goes wild!

~1ˢᵗ Grade
Classroom Management

The smallest student stood up and yelled out to the other students: "Yall know she is nice (referring to me), I mean she is way too nice to us and we won't listen! She is pretty and nice! I need us to really listen to Ms. Collier! She's not going to tell us again! This don't make any sense!"

Then he turns towards me and says, "You should be mean Ms. Collier! I'm serious, you need to be mean to us! You should try it! I bet'cha they'll listen!"

Student #1: "Yeah, Ms. Collier cause' moving them clips ain't doing nothing but you take them dollars (Ram Bucks) away and they gone get right!"

Smallest student: "If yall under me while I'm the helper, I'm taking dollars! Ain't that right Ms. Collier?"

Student #2: "Yall see this red marker?! We ain't playing!"

What more could I say?

~1st Grade
Straight to the TOP!

Teacher talking to student: "Go to the bathroom and blow your nose."
This baby went to the office and asked to call his mom to tell her to bring him some tissue...
In front of the principal!

~1st Grade
Career Day

The subject was about
obtaining a library card.

Student #1: "Can you put money
on the card?"
Presenter: "Not on this kind."

Student: "What?!
No money on the card?"

It was a total shocker to the class!

~1st Grade
I gotta go...

Student: "Ms. Collier, can I sit on the toilet?"

Ms. Collier: "Huh?

Student: "I ain't trying to ask you if I can sit on the toilet but I gotta sit on the toilet!

Ms. Collier: "Is your stomach hurting?"

Student: "YES! I gotta go!"

~1st Grade
2015 Slang

Student: "Ms. Collier! They singing that THOT song!"

Ms. Collier: "What's a THOT?"

Student: "You don't know what a THOT is?"

The way he looked at me made me pull out my urban dictionary and catch up!

~1st Grade
25th Day

Student: "Ms. Collier, today is my lucky day!"

Ms. Collier: "Why?"

Student: "Well, Fridays and the 25th are my lucky days!"

Me: "But why?"

Student: "Because Christmas is coming and Friday is coming!"

~1st Grade

<u>Forgetful teacher...</u>

"Ms. Collier, my birthday was December 3rd and you FORGOT! You celebrated everybody else's birthday and you forgot mine!" He gave me the ultimate sad face... All day!!

~1st Grade
We're sleepy!

Ms. Collier speaking to the class during our carpet chat...

"Today, you all have been acting a bit differently than usual! Usually on Mondays, you all are very calm and quiet but today, yall are off the chain! What's going on babies? Talk to me..."

Student #1 raises his hand and says, "I had coffee!"
Student #2 yells out (literally), "I didn't have breakfast!"
Student #3 yells, "I'm sleepy!"
Student #4 says, "I'm tired!"
Students #5-9 yell, "I'm ready to go home!"

"My feet hurt!"
"My stomach is hurting!"
"Can you call my momma?"
"My head is hurting!"
That was the end of our Monday!

~1st Grade
I was a kid too....

Brainstorming during a writing activity, I tell the students about myself as a first grader. Half of the class gasped for air and jumped with excitement while exclaiming, "You were a kid?!!"

The looks on their faces when I showed them my 1st grade picture were PRICELESS!

~1st Grade
<u>Use your resources...</u>

Ms. Collier: "Lil boy, will you stop going from table to table trying to get answers? Try it on your own!!"

Student: "I'm trying to get knowledge!"

Ms. Collier: Drops the pencil!

~1st Grade

<u>My neck...</u>

Student shouting with his head tilted to the side: "Ms. Collier! MY NECK IS BROKE! What you want me to do?!"

Ms. Collier: "Have a seat on the floor so that we can discuss Harriet Tubman."

He just stared at me with his broke neck. ☺

~1st Grade
Time...

Student: "Ms. Collier, why do we have to come to school at night now?"

After explaining about daylight savings, she says "Ooooo, so she's not dressed yet? She needs to hurry up and put on her uniform and get here!" As she looks out the window waiting.

~1st Grade

I confess...

I sneezed and someone yelled, "Lawd Jesus, Bless her!"
So that opened a conversation about God.

Student #1 says: "The Lord love you when you make mistakes, just like last night, I made a mistake!"

He never told us the mistake....
I am assuming this was his opportunity for confession.
☺

~1st Grade
<u>Boys will be boys...</u>

Ms. Collier: "Sweetie, why did you tell her that you love her?"

Student: "She kept telling me that she loved me, so I was saying it back to her. I was just saying random stuff so she could leave me alone!"

The little darlin' was in love with him the entire year! They start so early!

~1st Grade
Sitting down...

"I'm just gonna sit here listen and learn some stuff about Georgia Washington Carver!"

Math

"Why do you need math?"
Before I could answer, another student yells out, "You NEED multiplication through life man!"
He replies, "Oohhh"

~1st Grade
<u>Brain farts...</u>

"Ms. Collier, something wrong with my brain!"
Ms. Collier: "What's wrong darling?"

"I think it's playing! It won't think!"

That explains it ;)

<u>Never too late...</u>

A student who would sleep daily in class for a few hours a day comes and says "Ms. Collier, I'm woke now! I'm up! I'm ready to learn!"
We only had a few days left in school before summer break! Smh.

~1st Grade
It's so hard to say goodbye...

Student 1: "My 1st grade year almost over! I'm really gonna miss you guys!"

Other student: "I'm gonna miss yall too!"

Other student: "I ain't gonna forget about yall!"

The entire class begins to hug each other! I love my babies!

~1st Grade
I'm telling...

Ms. Collier: "Please stop tattling on each other. You all are about to become 2nd graders and you will have to learn to resolve some issues on your own."

Student: "That's right! God don't like tattle tellers!"

Student #2: "Whistleblowers can do that! They get to tattle tell on people! But I'm not gonna be a whistleblower! I'm done!"

~1st Grade

It's a helicopter!

We were outside playing and a helicopter flew over...
Student yells "That's a jet!"

I reply, "No baby, that's a helicopter!"

Student: "Well, my sister dumb! She told me that's a jet!"

"Don't call her dumb! How old is she?"

Student: "She's 11... What do I call her then?"

~1st Grade
Cologne & Boys

Monday, we (the boys) had a discussion about cologne. One boy stated that he likes the very popular Tom Ford cologne. I agreed with him that it smells really good! I also asked, "What do you know about that cologne?" He asked was I going to get some... I told him "No."

A few days later, he walks in and I was intrigued and questioned who had on cologne (it was rather vibrant)? Two of the boys had on expensive cologne including Tom Ford! He says to me, "Ms. Collier, smell me! I got on that Tom Ford but I had to share it with my dad!"

~1st Grade
<u>Good Behavior</u>

Student: "Imma be good today
Ms. Collier!"

Ms. Collier: "I know you are. You'll be
real good watching everybody play
for Field Day!"

~1st Grade
You must be specific...

I told the students that it was going to be a quiet day. At least I thought I did! Well, apparently I didn't make it clear.

Student: "If you had just said IT WAS going to be a QUIET day then I would have closed my mouth BUT you didn't say that! You said to be quiet... And I WAS quiet for a little while!"

Ms. Collier: "Get away from me nowwwwwww!" ☺

~1st Grade

#HashTag Sticky Notes

Student drawing Elsa's castle…
Teacher: "What's around the castle?"

Student: "Ice!"

Teacher: "What color can you use to draw ice?"

Student: "Dark white!"
#5yearsold #imagination #elsascastle

"White people not African American! They can't be!"
#blackhistorymonth #1stgrade

"Mommy is so serious!"
#prek #4yearsold

"Ms. Collier, why did you take off your heels?"

Me: "I didn't want to walk the stairs in them."

Student: "When I wear my church heels, I don't want to walk either, so I know what you mean!"
#5thgrade #theywatcheverything

"Ms. Collier, you're an old teacher!"

Me: "What do you mean?"

"I saw your Instagram picture with you writing on a chalkboard!!!"
#oldschoolteacher #whitechalkhands

"I ain't tryint to hang out with the bad crew anymore! I need to pass this CRCT!"
#2daysbeforeschoolisout
#nevertoolate

"Do you have an iPad?"

Me: "Yes and an iPhone."

"I don't have one because I'm not a mommy ☹"
#4yearsold

~5th grade

One last time...

In the middle of the 5th grade promotion ceremony, a male student turns to me and ask "Ms. Collier, is that a new dress?"

"No, now turn around and be quiet!"

"Ms. Collier, why are you always looking mean? Your eyebrow always raised!"

"I'm not mean, I got it from my daddy."

"Ms. Collier, is THAT a new dress?"

"BOY! Turn around and hush!"

He eventually turned around slowly,
smiling......

~1st Grade

Happy!

Me: "It's Friday! It's the weekend class!"

Class: "YEYYYYY!" Cheering and jumping and shouting all at once.

Student #1: "Hey! Y'all don't say that! It's our teacher and I'm gonna miss her 'cause it's the weekend! Y'all supposed to be sad and miss her because she loves us! Y'all say y'all sorry!"

Class: "Awwww, we sorry Teacher! We won't be happy 'cause it's the weekend!"

Me: "It's ok, you all can be happy!"

Class: "OK!!! YEYYYYY, WE HAPPY AGAIN!"

Me: "Have a wonderful weekend darlins! I love you!"

Analogy

Ms. Latressa Crawford: "Complete the analogy, plants is to caterpillar as clothes is to_____?"

Student: "Cock-a-Roach!!!"

How in the world did the student come up with the answer 'Cock-a-roach'? I simply stood back in amazement and bewilderment with a "WHAT?!? HUH?!?" expression on my face. The correct answer was moth. A caterpillar, which is an insect, eats plants and a moth, which is also an insect, eats clothes. His experience was not associated with moths. It was associated with 'cock-a-roaches'. In trying to broaden his "horizon", it left him with a "WHAT?! HUH?!?" expression on his face. The more I tried to explain the more frustrated we both became. I was like "MOTH... A MOTH! You should know this! What aren't you getting?" I had to then step back.

Judgmental mental the act of judgment. Judgmental is the forming of an opinion, estimate, notion, or conclusion, as from circumstances presented to the mind. Only after probing the student for more information did I realize his rational (which by the way still didn't make sense to me). However, what I learned from his explanation was that our experiences are not the same and therefore our rationale/logic would not be as well. We judge so quickly of others and take for granted their struggles. We assume that their struggles are like ours, when the truth of the matter is that they SIMPLY ARE NOT! This assumption/judgment causes us to have frustration with others, in addition to intolerance and sometimes indifference. I assumed that this student would know about moths versus roaches because of the area in which we lived. I judged that the student would be knowledgeable and be able to grasp the concept after verbal explanation. It was only after I stepped back, realized that his experience was different from mine, got rid of my frustration and took a different approach (which was to show him a picture, etc) that he began to understand and relate. This broadened his knowledge and increased my level of tolerance and decreased my assumptions.

Let us be less judgmental of others and more understanding. Let us realize that our struggles are different and let us explore different avenues of reaching one another.

"Do not judge by appearances, but judge with right judgment." John 7:24

Red, Yellow, Black, & White

Students: "He's not Black!"
Ms. Latressa Crawford: "Yes, he is!
Black people come in all shades."
Students: "Yeah! And colors too!!"

As a child we sang the song, Jesus Loves Me, and the verse that I loved most was "Red, Yellow, Black, and White, we are precious in His sight..." It just seemed to roll off of my tongue and filled me with a peace. Even as an adult and I'm writing this, I have a smile on my face and my shoulders are jumping. It's because I know I am loved. God has no respect of person. He loves us all no matter what we've done and no matter the color of our skin. If God can love us in spite of, why can't we love ourselves or each other? Let us look past the outside appearance. What a wonderful world it would be!

"...Love your neighbor as yourself. There is no commandment greater than these." Mark 12:31

Acknowledgements

My AWESOME and FUNNY 2014-2015
First Grade Class. All 18 of them!

To my family:

Thank you for always being there!

To my Handsome Hunnie:

Thank you for keeping me uplifted and
thanks for listening!

To my Management Team:

The P.O.W.E.R Experience

Thanks for pushing me beyond the sky!

To my publishing team:

FreedomInk Publishing & 2ii

Here we go... Again ☺

To my Social Media family:

Thanks for being a great audience and allowing me to share and you LIKED!

To my STCLM Family:

Thanks for the PRAYERS!

To my Scott Family:

Thanks for keeping my babies encouraged!

Contributors

Thank you to those who contributed their stories to Sticky Notes Volume I.

Dr. Darcova Triplett

Ms. Latressa Crawford

My Morris Brown Sisters

#MBCEducatorsAreTheBest

Author Bio

Trinette L. Collier, a native of Los Angeles, California, is a nationally renowned educator, entrepreneur, and author. She is the eldest of five children born to the late Mr. Ivory Collier and Mrs. Carolyn Collier. Life as a military kid afforded her the opportunity to travel the world. It is through this that she gained life experience while living in different states, cities and overseas. Her exposure to different cultures and races has led her to value and appreciate her very adventurous childhood. It is also through these experiences that she has been able to connect with the world at large thus honoring her fathers' life's desire for his children.

Trinette received her B.S. in Early Childhood Education from Morris Brown College in Atlanta, Georgia and her M.Ed. in Curriculum Instruction from Coppin State University. She is currently an educator with the Atlanta Public Schools system. Along with her formal career, she's also a Celebration Stylist in which she owns and operates California Dreaming Events, LLC. In November 2013, Ms. Collier added to her notoriety and became a published author debuting her award winning book *Woman On Fire*. In 2016, she added to her success the release of her second book entitled *Sticky Notes: Volume 1*.

Trinette currently resides in Atlanta, Georgia. She is an active member of Strong Tower Christian Life Ministries. She enjoys being with her family and friends. She loves helping others, learning, exploring new ideas, spoken word, music, and dancing!

www.ingramcontent.com/pod-product-compliance
Lightning Source LLC
Chambersburg PA
CBHW061956040426
42447CB00010B/1779